England

by Kay Melchisedech Olson

Blue Earth Books

an imprint of Capstone Press
Mankato, Minnesota

Blue Earth Books are published by Capstone Press
151 Good Counsel Drive, P.O. Box 669, Mankato, Minnesota 56002
http://www.capstone-press.com

Library of Congress Cataloging-in-Publication Data
Olson, Kay Melchisedech.
    England / by Kay Melchisedech Olson.
    p.cm—(Many cultures, one world)
    Includes bibliographical references and index.
    Contents: Welcome to England—An English legend—City and country life—Seasons in England—Family life in England—Laws, rules,
and customs—Pets in England—Sites to see in England.
    ISBN 0–7368–1532–5 (hardcover)
    1. England—Juvenile literature. [1. England.] I. Title. II. Series.
DA27.5 .046 2003
942—dc21   2002011888

    Summary: An introduction to the geography, history, economy, culture, and people of England, including a map, legend, recipe, craft, and game.

Editorial credits
Editor: Katy Kudela
Series Designer: Kia Adams
Photo Researcher: Jo Miller
Product Planning Editor: Karen Risch

Cover photo of London, England, by PictureQuest

Artistic effects
Photosphere

Capstone Press wishes to thank Dewi Williams from the British
Consulate-General in New York for his assistance in preparing
this book.

1 2 3 4 5 6 08 07 06 05 04 03

Photo credits
Bruce Coleman, Inc., 16–17; Ernest Janes, 6, 29 (right); W.H. Black, 14, 18;
    Larry Allan, 27 (right)
Capstone Press/Gary Sundermeyer, 3, 15, 19, 21 (right), 25, back cover
Corbis/Christie's Images, 8–9; Bettmann, 10; AFP, 17 (right); Patrick
    Ward, 20–21; Chris Jones, 26–27
Getty Images/UK Press, 22
Houserstock/Dave G. Houser, 12–13
Hulton/Archive by Getty Images, 11
The Image Finders/Bruce Leighty, 13 (right)
One Mile Up, Inc., 24 (top)
PhotoDisc, 28, 29 (left)
Photosphere, 4–5
Provided by: Audrius Tomonis-www.banknotes.com, 24 (bottom)
TRIP/H. Rogers, 23

Contents

Chapter 1

Welcome to England 4

Chapter 2

An English Legend 8

Chapter 3

City and Country Life 12

Chapter 4

Seasons in England 16

Chapter 5

Family Life in England 20

Chapter 6

Laws, Rules, and Customs 22

Chapter 7

Pets in England 26

Chapter 8

Sites to See in England 28

Words to Know 30

To Learn More 30

Useful Addresses 31

Internet Sites 31

Index 32

Turn to page 7 to find a map of England.

Find out how to make an English pudding on page 15.

Learn how to play a favorite English card game on page 19.

Check out page 25 to find out how people in England use crackers to celebrate Christmas.

CHAPTER 1

Welcome to England

England is a country of royalty. Kings and queens have ruled England for more than a thousand years. Today, Queen Elizabeth II is England's head of state. Buckingham Palace in London is one of her homes.

Royal Guards have guarded England's kings and queens for more than 300 years. These special guards wear red jackets and black bearskin hats. Foot Guards act out a ceremony called Guard Mounting.

Facts about England

Name: ....England (part of the United Kingdom)

Capital: ....London

Population: ....50 million people

Size: ....50,333 square miles

..........................(130,362 square kilometers)

Language: ....English

Religions: ....Anglican, Roman Catholic, Muslim

Highest point: ...Scafell Pike, 3,210 feet

..........................(978 meters) above sea level

Lowest point: ....the Fens, 15 feet (4.6 meters)

..........................below sea level

Main crops: ....Barley, wheat, oilseed, potatoes

Money: ....Pound sterling

Foot Guards march in front of Buckingham Palace to protect the queen and her family. The guards are trained not to smile while on duty.

Rolling hills make up most of England's countryside. High hills called the Pennine Chain run through northern England. The country's Lake District is north and west of the Pennines.

Low hills covered with marsh grass and heather are called moors.

Located to the east of the Pennines are the North York Moors. England's Lowlands are lands located south of the Pennines.

The southern part of England borders the English Channel. This body of water separates England from France.

England's countryside is covered with many low, rolling hills.

Map of England

SCOTLAND

NORTHERN
IRELAND

LAKE DISTRICT

NORTH YORK
MOORS

North Sea

*Scafell
Pike*

*P e n n i n e
C h a i n*

IRELAND

Irish Sea

WALES

Fens

ENGLAND

Thames River

⭐ London

English Channel

FRANCE

Legend
⭐ Capital City
🏔 Highest Point
ᴠ Lowest Point
〜 River

CHAPTER 2

An English Legend

Robin Hood was an outlaw in English legends. No one knows for sure if he was a real person. He may have been a made-up character. Legends are stories that often teach people something. Legends often are based on fact but are not always true.

Long ago, people wrote poems about a man they called Robin Hood. These poems are called ballads. They tell us much of what is known about Robin Hood.

Legends say Robin Hood and his Merry Men lived in Sherwood Forest.

The Legend of Robin Hood

Long ago on a sunny May morning, a young man named Robin Hood was on his way to the Nottingham Fair. Robin Hood was excellent at shooting a bow and arrows. He hoped to win the Sheriff's arrow shooting contest. He planned to use the prize money to buy a house and marry his girlfriend, Maid Marian.

On his way, Robin Hood met some soldiers. He knew the Sheriff's men enjoyed making trouble.

"Where are you going?" one of the soldiers asked.

"I am off to the fair to prove I am the best shot in all of England," Robin Hood answered.

The soldiers laughed. "Prove to us that you can shoot," one man said, pointing to a deer deep in Sherwood Forest.

Robin Hood knew that all forest animals belonged to the King. The Sheriff of Nottingham said anyone who shot one of the King's animals would be put to death.

"I cannot shoot the King's deer," Robin Hood said.

"So you are afraid," the soldier teased.

The soldier dared Robin Hood to shoot the deer. Robin Hood aimed his bow and arrow. He killed the deer with one shot. Then he ran deep into Sherwood Forest. He knew he could not go home. The soldiers would put him in jail. The Sheriff would have him killed. Robin Hood had to live in hiding in Sherwood Forest forever.

Robin Hood was an excellent hunter. He used a bow and arrows to hunt deer.

Robin Hood's friends soon joined him in the trees of Sherwood Forest. They wore green suits to make themselves harder to be seen against the leaves. Later, Maid Marian joined Robin Hood and his Merry Men in Sherwood Forest. They practiced shooting with bows and arrows. They killed deer in the King's forest. They played games and told stories.

One day a tax collector was riding near Sherwood Forest. He had taken the last few pennies from the poor people of Nottingham. Robin Hood and his men swooped down and stole the tax collector's bag of money. Later, they went in secret to return the money to the poor people of Nottingham.

Robin Hood, Maid Marian, and the Merry Men lived in Sherwood Forest for many years. They spent their days robbing from the rich to give to the poor.

People often came to Robin Hood for help. He became known as a hero throughout the country.

CHAPTER 3

City and Country Life

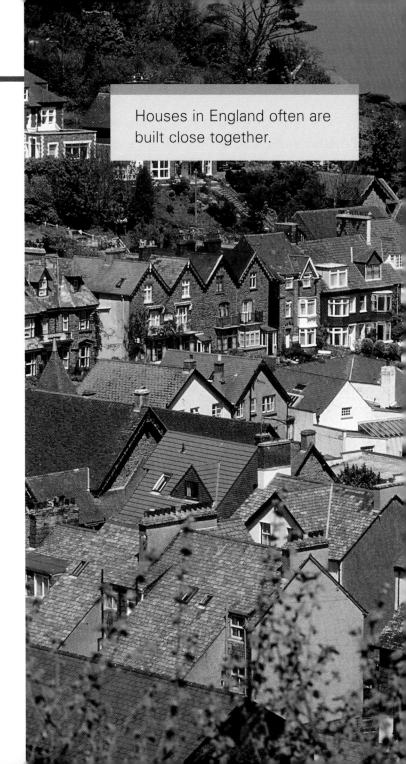

Houses in England often are built close together.

England is a little bigger than the U.S. state of Louisiana. But it has more than twice the number of people within its borders.

Most people in England live in cities. Some people live in apartments, and others live in houses.

In cities, many people travel by car. Some people travel by bus. England is famous for double-decker buses. A staircase inside the bus allows riders to choose a seat on the upper level. In London, people also ride the subway. They call this underground train "the tube."

In England, many people travel by bus. These red double-decker buses offer two levels of seating.

Subway trains run through narrow tubelike tunnels below the city.

Some of England's people live in rural areas. Many people who live in the country work on farms. Others live in the country but work in cities. These people travel to and from work by car or train.

The land in England's countryside gives farmers room to raise cattle and grow crops, such as wheat and barley.

Hasty Pudding

Hasty pudding is a tasty dessert. It earned its name because it can be made quickly. Someone who is in haste, or in a hurry, can make this dessert in a short amount of time.

What You Need

Ingredients

1 cup (240 mL) brown sugar
1 cup (240 mL) boiling water
1 teaspoon (5 mL) vanilla
2 tablespoons (30 mL) butter
½ cup (120 mL) sugar
¾ cup (175 mL) flour
½ cup (120 mL) milk
1 teaspoon (5 mL) baking powder
¾ cup (175 mL) chopped walnuts*
½ cup (120 mL) raisins*
(*optional)

Equipment

non-stick cooking
   spray
9-inch (23-centimeter)
   square baking dish
two medium bowls

dry-ingredient
   measuring cups
measuring spoons
liquid measuring cup
two mixing spoons

What You Do

1. Preheat oven to 350°F (180°C).
2. Apply non-stick cooking spray to the inside of the baking dish according to product directions. Set aside.
3. In one bowl, mix together brown sugar, boiling water, vanilla, and butter.
4. Pour the mixture into the baking dish.
5. In a second bowl, mix together sugar, flour, milk, and baking powder. Mix in chopped nuts and raisins if desired.
6. Drop this mixture by spoonfuls on top of the mixture in the baking dish.
7. Bake for 30 minutes.
8. Serve warm.

Makes about 4 large servings

CHAPTER 4

Seasons in England

None of England's four seasons have very hot or very cold temperatures. Every place in England is no more than 75 miles (121 kilometers) from the sea. Ocean winds bring fog to England during spring, summer, fall, and winter.

England rarely has heavy snowfall, but rain falls often in all four seasons. The area north and west of the Pennines gets the most rain. An average of 130 inches (330 centimeters) of rain falls there each year.

Rainy days are so common in England that people often ride bicycles to and from work in spite of the weather.

Brollies

Umbrellas are a familiar sight in England. People give umbrellas the nickname "brollies." English people carry umbrellas almost every day. Storms from the ocean come quickly and often without warning.

England is located north of the equator. This imaginary line circles Earth halfway between the North and South Poles.

Wind from the equator blows across the Atlantic Ocean to England. This air brings mild temperatures in winter.

England's winter temperatures average 40 degrees Fahrenheit (4.4 degrees Celsius).

Wind from the equator brings cool breezes in summer. Summer temperatures in England average 60 degrees Fahrenheit (15.6 degrees Celsius).

People in England can enjoy many outdoor activities. Temperatures are seldom very hot or very cold.

Play Snip, Snap, Snorem

Children in England often play indoor games on rainy days. Snip, Snap, Snorem is a favorite card game in England. People play with a deck of 12 different matched sets of four cards. You can play this game with a regular deck of 52 playing cards.

What You Need

four to six players
one deck of 52 playing cards

What You Do

1. Shuffle the cards and deal them to the players all face down. It does not matter if some players have more cards than the others do.
2. Players look at their own cards and hold them so no one else can see them.
3. The dealer chooses one of the cards he or she is holding and places it face up in the center.
4. The player on the left goes next. If this player has a matching card he or she places it on top of the first card and says "Snip." If the player does not have a matching card, it is the next player's turn.
5. The second person to hold a matching card lays it down and says "Snap."
6. The third person to hold a matching card lays it down and says "Snorem."
7. The last person to put down a card gets to start the next round by choosing any card and putting it face down on the pile.
8. The first player to run out of cards is the winner.

CHAPTER 5

Family Life in England

Most of England's families are small. Families usually have two parents and one or two children. About one-quarter of England's families have only one parent. Mothers most often head single-parent families. Almost half of the women in England work outside the home.

Gardening is a popular pastime in England. Most families grow flowers around their home. Many English homes have vegetable gardens in the backyard.

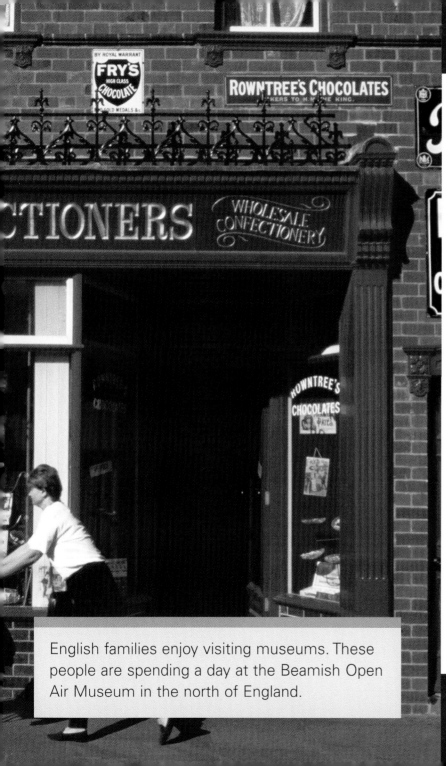

English families enjoy visiting museums. These people are spending a day at the Beamish Open Air Museum in the north of England.

Birthday Parties in England

Children in England often celebrate their birthdays with a fortune-telling cake. This cake is made with several small items baked inside it.

Whatever item is found in a slice is said to tell the fortune of the person eating it. The person who finds a coin in a cake slice may expect to become rich. The person who finds a marble in a cake slice may have good luck when playing games.

CHAPTER 6

Laws, Rules, and Customs

England is one of four countries that make up the United Kingdom. The other three members are Wales, Scotland, and Northern Ireland. The Irish Sea separates Northern Ireland from the rest of the United Kingdom.

Laws passed by Parliament govern the United Kingdom. Queen Elizabeth II is the United Kingdom's head of state. She is an important part of many ceremonies in England.

Queen Elizabeth II is the United Kingdom's head of state. She has been queen for more than 50 years.

Guy Fawkes Day

Every November 5, people in England celebrate Guy Fawkes Day. This day remembers a time in 1605 when a man named Guy Fawkes led a plot to blow up England's Parliament building. He and his group of followers wanted to kill King James I and the king's leaders. Guy Fawkes and his group were captured and put in prison before they were able to do harm.

People in England celebrate Guy Fawkes Day with fireworks and bonfires. Some people make Guy Fawkes dummies. Children wearing costumes and masks carry the straw dummies as they run up and down the streets. They shout, "A penny for the guy," and people give them money. Later, they throw the straw dummies into the bonfire.

Children enjoy the Guy Fawkes holiday in England. They make dummies stuffed with straw. At night they burn all the Guy Fawkes dummies in bonfires.

England's prime minister is the head of the government. The prime minister oversees the day-to-day business of England's government.

England's laws say that all children from the ages of 5 to 16 must attend school. The Department for Education and Skills is in charge of public schools.

Most English children attend public school. A small number of English children live at private boarding schools during the school term. They go home on weekends and holidays.

England's flag is a red cross on a white background. It is known as the St. George's Flag. St. George is the patron saint of England. Richard the Lionheart was crowned king in 1189. He chose the St. George's Flag to be England's official flag.

England's money is called the pound sterling. Both coins and paper money are used. One pound equals 100 pence.

Make a Christmas Cracker

Favorite prizes at Christmastime in England are Christmas crackers. A cracker is a small cardboard tube covered in brightly colored paper. Small candies, tiny toys, and other goodies are hidden inside the cracker.

You can make your own version of a Christmas cracker. Unlike the original, this cracker will not make a spark or a noise. But you can hide surprises inside for a friend to find.

What You Need

empty toilet paper roll
10-inch (25-centimeter) square piece of crepe paper
    or tissue-type wrapping paper
tape or glue
two lengths of ribbon about 8 inches
    (20 centimeters) long
items for the inside of the cracker (small candies,
    balloons, tiny toys, or other surprises)
stickers or marking pens

What You Do

1. Wrap the square of paper around the roll with an even amount on each side of the tube.
2. Tape or glue the edge of the paper so it does not unroll.
3. Tie one piece of ribbon around the paper at one end of the tube.
4. Fill the inside of the tube with items through the open end of the paper.
5. Tie the second piece of ribbon around the paper to close the other end.
6. Use stickers or marking pens to decorate the paper covering the cracker.
7. Give the cracker to a friend for a special occasion.

CHAPTER 7

Pets in England

Dogs and cats are the most popular pets in England. About 5.3 million families in England own a dog and about 5 million own a cat.

The Labrador retriever is the most popular dog in England. The Persian longhair is the most popular cat in England.

Birds called budgerigars are popular pets in England. About 650,000 English people own these birds, which they call "budgies." Rabbits, goldfish, and guinea pigs are other popular pets.

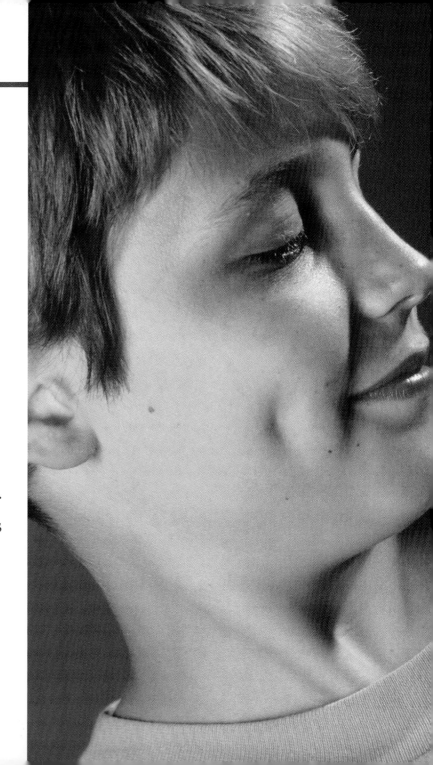

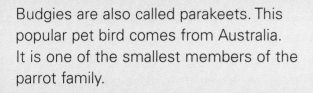

Budgies are also called parakeets. This popular pet bird comes from Australia. It is one of the smallest members of the parrot family.

Queen Elizabeth's Pets

Queen Elizabeth II has owned more than 30 Corgi dogs in her lifetime. Corgis have short legs and no tail. The Queen's first Corgi was named Susan.

Queen Elizabeth's family has also loved Corgis. Queen Elizabeth's father, King George VI, owned Corgis. Her sister, Princess Margaret, had both pet Corgis and Dachshunds. A Dachshund is a dog with short legs and a long body.

Princess Margaret once bred a Corgi with a Dachshund. She gave this new "Dorgi" dog the name Berry.

CHAPTER 8

Sites to See in England

London has more interesting sites to see than any other city in England. Many palaces and museums show the history of England's kings and queens. Buckingham Palace is the home and office of Queen Elizabeth II. Tourists who pay for tickets may visit certain rooms in Buckingham Palace. Visitors also can watch the Changing of the Guard ceremony outside the palace.

Big Ben and the Houses of Parliament are also in London. Big Ben is a huge bell

Tower Bridge crosses the Thames River in London.

in St. Stephen's Tower. The tower has a clock face on each of its four sides. Big Ben rings out each hour during the day and night. When the government is in session in the Houses of Parliament, a light shines above the clock faces.

Almost every site in London can be seen from a huge wheel on the edge of the Thames River. England's London Eye looks like a giant Ferris wheel. People in the cars ride about 500 feet (152 meters)

Visitors who pay for tickets on the London Eye may view London for 30 minutes as their viewing car travels around the wheel.

Stonehenge is located in southwestern England. No one is certain who placed the large stones in this arrangement.

above the ground. London Eye is the world's tallest viewing wheel.

Stonehenge is an interesting site in England's countryside. Stonehenge is a group of giant stone blocks. Scientists believe Stonehenge was built more than 3,000 years ago. More than 1 million tourists visit Stonehenge each year.

Words to Know

ballad (BAL-uhd)—a song or poem that tells a story

equator (e-KWAY-tur)—an imaginary line around Earth; the equator is halfway between the North and South Poles.

heather (HETH-ur)—a small bush with pink, purple, or white flowers

moor (MOR)—open, rolling land covered with coarse marsh grasses and low evergreen bushes of heather

outlaw (OUT-law)—a person who does not obey the law

Parliament (PAR-luh-muhnt)—the governing body that makes the laws in Britain

patron saint (PAY-truhn SAYNT)—a person honored by the Christian church for leading a holy life; some people believe a patron saint looks after a country or group of people; St. George is the patron saint of England.

To Learn More

Allport, Alan. *England.* Modern World Nations. Philadelphia: Chelsea House, 2002.

Deady, Kathleen W. *England.* Countries of the World. Mankato, Minn.: Bridgestone Books, 2001.

Ganeri, Anita. *England.* A Visit To. Chicago: Heinemann Library, 2003.

Hill, Barbara W. *Cooking the English Way.* Easy Menu Ethnic Cookbooks. Minneapolis: Lerner, 2002.

Useful Addresses

American Friends of the British Museum
One East 53rd Street
New York, NY 10022

British Embassy
3100 Massachusetts Avenue
Washington, DC 20008

The British Museum
Great Russell Street
London WC1B 3DG
England

British Tourist Authority
111 Avenue Road, Suite 450
Toronto, ON M5R 3J8
Canada

Internet Sites

Track down many sites about England.
Visit the FACT HOUND at *http://www.facthound.com*

IT IS EASY! IT IS FUN!

1) Go to *http://www.facthound.com*
2) Type in: 0736815325
3) Click on "FETCH IT" and FACT HOUND will find several links hand-picked by our editors.

Relax and let our pal FACT HOUND do the research for you!

Index

Big Ben, 28–29
birthday. See celebration
Buckingham Palace, 4, 5, 28
budgerigars. See pets

celebration, 21, 23, 25
children, 20, 21, 23, 24
Christmas. See celebration
Corgi, 27
countryside, 6, 14, 29
crops, 5, 14

Elizabeth II (Queen of England), 4, 5, 22, 27, 28

family, 5, 20, 21, 26
Fens, 5
flag, 24
food, 15, 21
Foot Guards, 4, 5

gardens, 20
government, 22, 24, 29
Guard Mounting, 4
Guy Fawkes Day. See celebration

Hood, Robin, 8, 10–11
Houses of Parliament, 28–29
housing, 12

Lake District, 6
legend, 8, 10–11
London, 4, 5, 12, 28, 29
London Eye, 29

Maid Marian, 10, 11
Merry Men, 8, 11
money, 5, 24
moors, 6

North York Moors. See moors

Parliament, 22
Pennine Chain, 6, 16
pets, 26, 27
population, 5, 12
prime minister, 24
pudding. See food

rain, 16
religion, 5
Royal Guards, 4

Scafell Pike, 5
school, 24
seasons, 16, 18
Stonehenge, 29

Thames River, 28, 29
transportation, 12, 13, 14, 16

umbrellas, 17
United Kingdom, 5, 22

weather, 16, 17, 18